THIS BOOK BELONGS TO:

CONTACT INFORMATION	
NAME:	
ADDRESS:	
PHONE:	

START / END DATES

_____ / _____ / _____   TO   _____ / _____ / _____

Dedication

This Order Log Book is dedicated to all the small or home-based businesses out there who want to keep their customer order notes organized and document their findings in the process.

You are my inspiration for producing books and I'm honored to be a part of keeping all of your order notes and records organized.

This journal notebook will help you record the details of your business's customer orders.

Thoughtfully put together with these sections to record: Customer Info, Order # & Status, Date & Payment Method, Shipped or Canceled, Est Shipping Date, Shipping Company, Tracking, Shipping Date, Arrival Date, Notes, and much more!

How to Use this Book

The purpose of this book is to keep all of your Order notes all in one place. It will help keep you organized.

This Order Log Book will allow you to accurately document details about your customer orders.

Here are examples of the prompts for you to fill in and write about your experience in this book:

1. Customer Name, Address, Phone & E-mail.

2. Order Number & Status

3. Date & Payment Method

4. Shipped or Canceled

5. Estimated Shipping Date, Shipping Company, Tracking, Shipping Date, & Arrival Date.

6. Item # & Description

7. Quantity, Price & Final Price

8. Subtotal, Discount, Taxes, Shipping, and Grand Total

9. Notes

Order Form

ORDER #	
DATE	

CUSTOMER	
ADDRESS	
PHONE	
EMAIL	

STATUS	
o PAID / METHOD	
o SHIPPED	
o CANCELLED	
EST. SHIPPING DATE	
SHIPPING COMPANY	
TRACKING	
SHIPPING DATE	
ARRIVAL DATE	

ITEM #	DESCRIPTION	QTY	PRICE	FINAL PRICE

NOTES	SUBTOTAL	
	DISCOUNT	
	TAXES	
	SHIPPING	
	GRAND TOTAL	

Order Form

ORDER #	
DATE	

CUSTOMER	
ADDRESS	
PHONE	
EMAIL	

STATUS	
o PAID / METHOD	
o SHIPPED	
o CANCELLED	
EST. SHIPPING DATE	
SHIPPING COMPANY	
TRACKING	
SHIPPING DATE	
ARRIVAL DATE	

ITEM #	DESCRIPTION	QTY	PRICE	FINAL PRICE

NOTES		SUBTOTAL	
		DISCOUNT	
		TAXES	
		SHIPPING	
		GRAND TOTAL	

Order Form

ORDER #	
DATE	

CUSTOMER	
ADDRESS	
PHONE	
EMAIL	

STATUS	
o PAID / METHOD	
o SHIPPED	
o CANCELLED	
EST. SHIPPING DATE	
SHIPPING COMPANY	
TRACKING	
SHIPPING DATE	
ARRIVAL DATE	

ITEM #	DESCRIPTION	QTY	PRICE	FINAL PRICE

NOTES		SUBTOTAL	
		DISCOUNT	
		TAXES	
		SHIPPING	
		GRAND TOTAL	

Order Form

ORDER #	
DATE	

CUSTOMER	
ADDRESS	
PHONE	
EMAIL	

STATUS	
o PAID / METHOD	
o SHIPPED	
o CANCELLED	
EST. SHIPPING DATE	
SHIPPING COMPANY	
TRACKING	
SHIPPING DATE	
ARRIVAL DATE	

ITEM #	DESCRIPTION	QTY	PRICE	FINAL PRICE

NOTES	SUBTOTAL	
	DISCOUNT	
	TAXES	
	SHIPPING	
	GRAND TOTAL	

Order Form

ORDER #	
DATE	

CUSTOMER	
ADDRESS	
PHONE	
EMAIL	

STATUS	
o PAID / METHOD	
o SHIPPED	
o CANCELLED	
EST. SHIPPING DATE	
SHIPPING COMPANY	
TRACKING	
SHIPPING DATE	
ARRIVAL DATE	

ITEM #	DESCRIPTION	QTY	PRICE	FINAL PRICE

NOTES	SUBTOTAL	
	DISCOUNT	
	TAXES	
	SHIPPING	
	GRAND TOTAL	

Order Form

ORDER #	
DATE	

CUSTOMER	
ADDRESS	
PHONE	
EMAIL	

STATUS	
o PAID / METHOD	
o SHIPPED	
o CANCELLED	
EST. SHIPPING DATE	
SHIPPING COMPANY	
TRACKING	
SHIPPING DATE	
ARRIVAL DATE	

ITEM #	DESCRIPTION	QTY	PRICE	FINAL PRICE

NOTES		SUBTOTAL	
		DISCOUNT	
		TAXES	
		SHIPPING	
		GRAND TOTAL	

Order Form

ORDER #		STATUS	
DATE		o PAID / METHOD	
CUSTOMER		o SHIPPED	
		o CANCELLED	
ADDRESS		EST. SHIPPING DATE	
		SHIPPING COMPANY	
PHONE		TRACKING	
		SHIPPING DATE	
EMAIL		ARRIVAL DATE	

ITEM #	DESCRIPTION	QTY	PRICE	FINAL PRICE

NOTES	SUBTOTAL	
	DISCOUNT	
	TAXES	
	SHIPPING	
	GRAND TOTAL	

Order Form

ORDER #	
DATE	

CUSTOMER	
ADDRESS	
PHONE	
EMAIL	

STATUS	
o PAID / METHOD	
o SHIPPED	
o CANCELLED	
EST. SHIPPING DATE	
SHIPPING COMPANY	
TRACKING	
SHIPPING DATE	
ARRIVAL DATE	

ITEM #	DESCRIPTION	QTY	PRICE	FINAL PRICE

NOTES	SUBTOTAL	
	DISCOUNT	
	TAXES	
	SHIPPING	
	GRAND TOTAL	

Order Form

ORDER #	
DATE	

CUSTOMER	
ADDRESS	
PHONE	
EMAIL	

STATUS	
o PAID / METHOD	
o SHIPPED	
o CANCELLED	
EST. SHIPPING DATE	
SHIPPING COMPANY	
TRACKING	
SHIPPING DATE	
ARRIVAL DATE	

ITEM #	DESCRIPTION	QTY	PRICE	FINAL PRICE

NOTES	

SUBTOTAL	
DISCOUNT	
TAXES	
SHIPPING	
GRAND TOTAL	

Order Form

ORDER #	
DATE	

STATUS	
o PAID / METHOD	
o SHIPPED	
o CANCELLED	

CUSTOMER	
ADDRESS	
PHONE	
EMAIL	

EST. SHIPPING DATE	
SHIPPING COMPANY	
TRACKING	
SHIPPING DATE	
ARRIVAL DATE	

ITEM #	DESCRIPTION	QTY	PRICE	FINAL PRICE

NOTES

SUBTOTAL	
DISCOUNT	
TAXES	
SHIPPING	
GRAND TOTAL	

Order Form

ORDER #	
DATE	

CUSTOMER	
ADDRESS	
PHONE	
EMAIL	

STATUS	
o PAID / METHOD	
o SHIPPED	
o CANCELLED	
EST. SHIPPING DATE	
SHIPPING COMPANY	
TRACKING	
SHIPPING DATE	
ARRIVAL DATE	

ITEM #	DESCRIPTION	QTY	PRICE	FINAL PRICE

NOTES	SUBTOTAL	
	DISCOUNT	
	TAXES	
	SHIPPING	
	GRAND TOTAL	

Order Form

ORDER #	
DATE	

CUSTOMER	
ADDRESS	
PHONE	
EMAIL	

STATUS	
o PAID / METHOD	
o SHIPPED	
o CANCELLED	
EST. SHIPPING DATE	
SHIPPING COMPANY	
TRACKING	
SHIPPING DATE	
ARRIVAL DATE	

ITEM #	DESCRIPTION	QTY	PRICE	FINAL PRICE

NOTES	SUBTOTAL	
	DISCOUNT	
	TAXES	
	SHIPPING	
	GRAND TOTAL	

Order Form

ORDER #	
DATE	

CUSTOMER	
ADDRESS	
PHONE	
EMAIL	

STATUS	
o PAID / METHOD	
o SHIPPED	
o CANCELLED	
EST. SHIPPING DATE	
SHIPPING COMPANY	
TRACKING	
SHIPPING DATE	
ARRIVAL DATE	

ITEM #	DESCRIPTION	QTY	PRICE	FINAL PRICE

NOTES

SUBTOTAL	
DISCOUNT	
TAXES	
SHIPPING	
GRAND TOTAL	

Order Form

ORDER #	
DATE	

CUSTOMER	
ADDRESS	
PHONE	
EMAIL	

STATUS	
o PAID / METHOD	
o SHIPPED	
o CANCELLED	
EST. SHIPPING DATE	
SHIPPING COMPANY	
TRACKING	
SHIPPING DATE	
ARRIVAL DATE	

ITEM #	DESCRIPTION	QTY	PRICE	FINAL PRICE

NOTES	

SUBTOTAL	
DISCOUNT	
TAXES	
SHIPPING	
GRAND TOTAL	

Order Form

ORDER #	
DATE	

CUSTOMER	
ADDRESS	
PHONE	
EMAIL	

STATUS	
o PAID / METHOD	
o SHIPPED	
o CANCELLED	
EST. SHIPPING DATE	
SHIPPING COMPANY	
TRACKING	
SHIPPING DATE	
ARRIVAL DATE	

ITEM #	DESCRIPTION	QTY	PRICE	FINAL PRICE

NOTES		SUBTOTAL	
		DISCOUNT	
		TAXES	
		SHIPPING	
		GRAND TOTAL	

Order Form

ORDER #	
DATE	

CUSTOMER	
ADDRESS	
PHONE	
EMAIL	

STATUS	
o PAID / METHOD	
o SHIPPED	
o CANCELLED	
EST. SHIPPING DATE	
SHIPPING COMPANY	
TRACKING	
SHIPPING DATE	
ARRIVAL DATE	

ITEM #	DESCRIPTION	QTY	PRICE	FINAL PRICE

NOTES	SUBTOTAL	
	DISCOUNT	
	TAXES	
	SHIPPING	
	GRAND TOTAL	

Order Form

ORDER #	
DATE	

CUSTOMER	
ADDRESS	
PHONE	
EMAIL	

STATUS	
o PAID / METHOD	
o SHIPPED	
o CANCELLED	
EST. SHIPPING DATE	
SHIPPING COMPANY	
TRACKING	
SHIPPING DATE	
ARRIVAL DATE	

ITEM #	DESCRIPTION	QTY	PRICE	FINAL PRICE

NOTES		SUBTOTAL	
		DISCOUNT	
		TAXES	
		SHIPPING	
		GRAND TOTAL	

Order Form

ORDER #	
DATE	

CUSTOMER	
ADDRESS	
PHONE	
EMAIL	

STATUS	
o PAID / METHOD	
o SHIPPED	
o CANCELLED	
EST. SHIPPING DATE	
SHIPPING COMPANY	
TRACKING	
SHIPPING DATE	
ARRIVAL DATE	

ITEM #	DESCRIPTION	QTY	PRICE	FINAL PRICE

NOTES		SUBTOTAL	
		DISCOUNT	
		TAXES	
		SHIPPING	
		GRAND TOTAL	

Order Form

ORDER #	
DATE	

CUSTOMER	
ADDRESS	
PHONE	
EMAIL	

STATUS	
o PAID / METHOD	
o SHIPPED	
o CANCELLED	
EST. SHIPPING DATE	
SHIPPING COMPANY	
TRACKING	
SHIPPING DATE	
ARRIVAL DATE	

ITEM #	DESCRIPTION	QTY	PRICE	FINAL PRICE

NOTES	SUBTOTAL	
	DISCOUNT	
	TAXES	
	SHIPPING	
	GRAND TOTAL	

Order Form

ORDER #	
DATE	

CUSTOMER	
ADDRESS	
PHONE	
EMAIL	

STATUS	
o PAID / METHOD	
o SHIPPED	
o CANCELLED	
EST. SHIPPING DATE	
SHIPPING COMPANY	
TRACKING	
SHIPPING DATE	
ARRIVAL DATE	

ITEM #	DESCRIPTION	QTY	PRICE	FINAL PRICE

NOTES	SUBTOTAL	
	DISCOUNT	
	TAXES	
	SHIPPING	
	GRAND TOTAL	

Order Form

ORDER #		STATUS	
DATE		o PAID / METHOD	
CUSTOMER		o SHIPPED	
		o CANCELLED	
ADDRESS		EST. SHIPPING DATE	
		SHIPPING COMPANY	
PHONE		TRACKING	
		SHIPPING DATE	
EMAIL		ARRIVAL DATE	

ITEM #	DESCRIPTION	QTY	PRICE	FINAL PRICE

NOTES	SUBTOTAL	
	DISCOUNT	
	TAXES	
	SHIPPING	
	GRAND TOTAL	

Order Form

ORDER #	
DATE	

CUSTOMER	
ADDRESS	
PHONE	
EMAIL	

STATUS	
o PAID / METHOD	
o SHIPPED	
o CANCELLED	
EST. SHIPPING DATE	
SHIPPING COMPANY	
TRACKING	
SHIPPING DATE	
ARRIVAL DATE	

ITEM #	DESCRIPTION	QTY	PRICE	FINAL PRICE

NOTES		
	SUBTOTAL	
	DISCOUNT	
	TAXES	
	SHIPPING	
	GRAND TOTAL	

Order Form

ORDER #	
DATE	

CUSTOMER	
ADDRESS	
PHONE	
EMAIL	

STATUS	
o PAID / METHOD	
o SHIPPED	
o CANCELLED	
EST. SHIPPING DATE	
SHIPPING COMPANY	
TRACKING	
SHIPPING DATE	
ARRIVAL DATE	

ITEM #	DESCRIPTION	QTY	PRICE	FINAL PRICE

NOTES	SUBTOTAL	
	DISCOUNT	
	TAXES	
	SHIPPING	
	GRAND TOTAL	

Order Form

ORDER #	
DATE	

CUSTOMER	
ADDRESS	
PHONE	
EMAIL	

STATUS	
o PAID / METHOD	
o SHIPPED	
o CANCELLED	
EST. SHIPPING DATE	
SHIPPING COMPANY	
TRACKING	
SHIPPING DATE	
ARRIVAL DATE	

ITEM #	DESCRIPTION	QTY	PRICE	FINAL PRICE

NOTES	SUBTOTAL	
	DISCOUNT	
	TAXES	
	SHIPPING	
	GRAND TOTAL	

Order Form

ORDER #	
DATE	

CUSTOMER	
ADDRESS	
PHONE	
EMAIL	

STATUS	
o PAID / METHOD	
o SHIPPED	
o CANCELLED	
EST. SHIPPING DATE	
SHIPPING COMPANY	
TRACKING	
SHIPPING DATE	
ARRIVAL DATE	

ITEM #	DESCRIPTION	QTY	PRICE	FINAL PRICE

NOTES

SUBTOTAL	
DISCOUNT	
TAXES	
SHIPPING	
GRAND TOTAL	

Order Form

ORDER #	
DATE	

CUSTOMER	
ADDRESS	
PHONE	
EMAIL	

STATUS

- o PAID / METHOD
- o SHIPPED
- o CANCELLED

EST. SHIPPING DATE	
SHIPPING COMPANY	
TRACKING	
SHIPPING DATE	
ARRIVAL DATE	

ITEM #	DESCRIPTION	QTY	PRICE	FINAL PRICE

NOTES

SUBTOTAL	
DISCOUNT	
TAXES	
SHIPPING	
GRAND TOTAL	

Order Form

ORDER #	
DATE	

CUSTOMER	
ADDRESS	
PHONE	
EMAIL	

STATUS	
o PAID / METHOD	
o SHIPPED	
o CANCELLED	
EST. SHIPPING DATE	
SHIPPING COMPANY	
TRACKING	
SHIPPING DATE	
ARRIVAL DATE	

ITEM #	DESCRIPTION	QTY	PRICE	FINAL PRICE

NOTES

SUBTOTAL	
DISCOUNT	
TAXES	
SHIPPING	
GRAND TOTAL	

Order Form

ORDER #	
DATE	

CUSTOMER	
ADDRESS	
PHONE	
EMAIL	

STATUS	
o PAID / METHOD	
o SHIPPED	
o CANCELLED	
EST. SHIPPING DATE	
SHIPPING COMPANY	
TRACKING	
SHIPPING DATE	
ARRIVAL DATE	

ITEM #	DESCRIPTION	QTY	PRICE	FINAL PRICE

NOTES	SUBTOTAL	
	DISCOUNT	
	TAXES	
	SHIPPING	
	GRAND TOTAL	

Order Form

ORDER #	
DATE	

CUSTOMER	
ADDRESS	
PHONE	
EMAIL	

STATUS	
o PAID / METHOD	
o SHIPPED	
o CANCELLED	
EST. SHIPPING DATE	
SHIPPING COMPANY	
TRACKING	
SHIPPING DATE	
ARRIVAL DATE	

ITEM #	DESCRIPTION	QTY	PRICE	FINAL PRICE

NOTES	SUBTOTAL	
	DISCOUNT	
	TAXES	
	SHIPPING	
	GRAND TOTAL	

Order Form

ORDER #	
DATE	

CUSTOMER	
ADDRESS	
PHONE	
EMAIL	

STATUS	
o PAID / METHOD	
o SHIPPED	
o CANCELLED	
EST. SHIPPING DATE	
SHIPPING COMPANY	
TRACKING	
SHIPPING DATE	
ARRIVAL DATE	

ITEM #	DESCRIPTION	QTY	PRICE	FINAL PRICE

NOTES	SUBTOTAL	
	DISCOUNT	
	TAXES	
	SHIPPING	
	GRAND TOTAL	

Order Form

ORDER #		STATUS	
DATE		o PAID / METHOD	
CUSTOMER		o SHIPPED	
		o CANCELLED	
ADDRESS		EST. SHIPPING DATE	
		SHIPPING COMPANY	
PHONE		TRACKING	
		SHIPPING DATE	
EMAIL		ARRIVAL DATE	

ITEM #	DESCRIPTION	QTY	PRICE	FINAL PRICE

NOTES			
	SUBTOTAL	
	DISCOUNT	
	TAXES	
	SHIPPING	
	GRAND TOTAL	

Order Form

ORDER #	
DATE	

CUSTOMER	
ADDRESS	
PHONE	
EMAIL	

STATUS	
o PAID / METHOD	
o SHIPPED	
o CANCELLED	
EST. SHIPPING DATE	
SHIPPING COMPANY	
TRACKING	
SHIPPING DATE	
ARRIVAL DATE	

ITEM #	DESCRIPTION	QTY	PRICE	FINAL PRICE

NOTES		
	SUBTOTAL	
	DISCOUNT	
	TAXES	
	SHIPPING	
	GRAND TOTAL	

Order Form

ORDER #	
DATE	

CUSTOMER	
ADDRESS	
PHONE	
EMAIL	

STATUS	
o PAID / METHOD	
o SHIPPED	
o CANCELLED	
EST. SHIPPING DATE	
SHIPPING COMPANY	
TRACKING	
SHIPPING DATE	
ARRIVAL DATE	

ITEM #	DESCRIPTION	QTY	PRICE	FINAL PRICE

NOTES

SUBTOTAL	
DISCOUNT	
TAXES	
SHIPPING	
GRAND TOTAL	

Order Form

ORDER #	
DATE	

CUSTOMER	
ADDRESS	
PHONE	
EMAIL	

STATUS	
o PAID / METHOD	
o SHIPPED	
o CANCELLED	
EST. SHIPPING DATE	
SHIPPING COMPANY	
TRACKING	
SHIPPING DATE	
ARRIVAL DATE	

ITEM #	DESCRIPTION	QTY	PRICE	FINAL PRICE

NOTES

SUBTOTAL	
DISCOUNT	
TAXES	
SHIPPING	
GRAND TOTAL	

Order Form

ORDER #	
DATE	

CUSTOMER	
ADDRESS	
PHONE	
EMAIL	

STATUS	
o PAID / METHOD	
o SHIPPED	
o CANCELLED	
EST. SHIPPING DATE	
SHIPPING COMPANY	
TRACKING	
SHIPPING DATE	
ARRIVAL DATE	

ITEM #	DESCRIPTION	QTY	PRICE	FINAL PRICE

NOTES	SUBTOTAL	
	DISCOUNT	
	TAXES	
	SHIPPING	
	GRAND TOTAL	

Order Form

ORDER #	
DATE	

CUSTOMER	
ADDRESS	
PHONE	
EMAIL	

STATUS	
o PAID / METHOD	
o SHIPPED	
o CANCELLED	
EST. SHIPPING DATE	
SHIPPING COMPANY	
TRACKING	
SHIPPING DATE	
ARRIVAL DATE	

ITEM #	DESCRIPTION	QTY	PRICE	FINAL PRICE

NOTES	SUBTOTAL	
	DISCOUNT	
	TAXES	
	SHIPPING	
	GRAND TOTAL	

Order Form

ORDER #	
DATE	

CUSTOMER	
ADDRESS	
PHONE	
EMAIL	

STATUS	
o PAID / METHOD	
o SHIPPED	
o CANCELLED	
EST. SHIPPING DATE	
SHIPPING COMPANY	
TRACKING	
SHIPPING DATE	
ARRIVAL DATE	

ITEM #	DESCRIPTION	QTY	PRICE	FINAL PRICE

NOTES		SUBTOTAL	
		DISCOUNT	
		TAXES	
		SHIPPING	
		GRAND TOTAL	

Order Form

ORDER #	
DATE	

CUSTOMER	
ADDRESS	
PHONE	
EMAIL	

STATUS	
o PAID / METHOD	
o SHIPPED	
o CANCELLED	
EST. SHIPPING DATE	
SHIPPING COMPANY	
TRACKING	
SHIPPING DATE	
ARRIVAL DATE	

ITEM #	DESCRIPTION	QTY	PRICE	FINAL PRICE

NOTES	SUBTOTAL	
	DISCOUNT	
	TAXES	
	SHIPPING	
	GRAND TOTAL	

Order Form

ORDER #	
DATE	

CUSTOMER	
ADDRESS	
PHONE	
EMAIL	

STATUS	
o PAID / METHOD	
o SHIPPED	
o CANCELLED	
EST. SHIPPING DATE	
SHIPPING COMPANY	
TRACKING	
SHIPPING DATE	
ARRIVAL DATE	

ITEM #	DESCRIPTION	QTY	PRICE	FINAL PRICE

NOTES

SUBTOTAL	
DISCOUNT	
TAXES	
SHIPPING	
GRAND TOTAL	

Order Form

ORDER #	
DATE	

CUSTOMER	
ADDRESS	
PHONE	
EMAIL	

STATUS	
o PAID / METHOD	
o SHIPPED	
o CANCELLED	
EST. SHIPPING DATE	
SHIPPING COMPANY	
TRACKING	
SHIPPING DATE	
ARRIVAL DATE	

ITEM #	DESCRIPTION	QTY	PRICE	FINAL PRICE

NOTES		SUBTOTAL	
		DISCOUNT	
		TAXES	
		SHIPPING	
		GRAND TOTAL	

Order Form

ORDER #	
DATE	

CUSTOMER	
ADDRESS	
PHONE	
EMAIL	

STATUS	
o PAID / METHOD	
o SHIPPED	
o CANCELLED	
EST. SHIPPING DATE	
SHIPPING COMPANY	
TRACKING	
SHIPPING DATE	
ARRIVAL DATE	

ITEM #	DESCRIPTION	QTY	PRICE	FINAL PRICE

NOTES

SUBTOTAL	
DISCOUNT	
TAXES	
SHIPPING	
GRAND TOTAL	

Order Form

ORDER #	
DATE	

CUSTOMER	
ADDRESS	
PHONE	
EMAIL	

STATUS	
o PAID / METHOD	
o SHIPPED	
o CANCELLED	
EST. SHIPPING DATE	
SHIPPING COMPANY	
TRACKING	
SHIPPING DATE	
ARRIVAL DATE	

ITEM #	DESCRIPTION	QTY	PRICE	FINAL PRICE

NOTES		SUBTOTAL	
		DISCOUNT	
		TAXES	
		SHIPPING	
		GRAND TOTAL	

Order Form

ORDER #		STATUS	
DATE		o PAID / METHOD	
CUSTOMER		o SHIPPED	
		o CANCELLED	
ADDRESS		EST. SHIPPING DATE	
		SHIPPING COMPANY	
PHONE		TRACKING	
		SHIPPING DATE	
EMAIL		ARRIVAL DATE	

ITEM #	DESCRIPTION	QTY	PRICE	FINAL PRICE

NOTES	SUBTOTAL	
	DISCOUNT	
	TAXES	
	SHIPPING	
	GRAND TOTAL	

Order Form

ORDER #	
DATE	

CUSTOMER	
ADDRESS	
PHONE	
EMAIL	

STATUS	
o PAID / METHOD	
o SHIPPED	
o CANCELLED	
EST. SHIPPING DATE	
SHIPPING COMPANY	
TRACKING	
SHIPPING DATE	
ARRIVAL DATE	

ITEM #	DESCRIPTION	QTY	PRICE	FINAL PRICE

NOTES

SUBTOTAL	
DISCOUNT	
TAXES	
SHIPPING	
GRAND TOTAL	

Order Form

ORDER #	
DATE	

CUSTOMER	
ADDRESS	
PHONE	
EMAIL	

STATUS	
o PAID / METHOD	
o SHIPPED	
o CANCELLED	
EST. SHIPPING DATE	
SHIPPING COMPANY	
TRACKING	
SHIPPING DATE	
ARRIVAL DATE	

ITEM #	DESCRIPTION	QTY	PRICE	FINAL PRICE

NOTES		SUBTOTAL	
		DISCOUNT	
		TAXES	
		SHIPPING	
		GRAND TOTAL	

Order Form

ORDER #	
DATE	

CUSTOMER	
ADDRESS	
PHONE	
EMAIL	

STATUS	
o PAID / METHOD	
o SHIPPED	
o CANCELLED	
EST. SHIPPING DATE	
SHIPPING COMPANY	
TRACKING	
SHIPPING DATE	
ARRIVAL DATE	

ITEM #	DESCRIPTION	QTY	PRICE	FINAL PRICE

NOTES		SUBTOTAL	
		DISCOUNT	
		TAXES	
		SHIPPING	
		GRAND TOTAL	

Order Form

ORDER #		STATUS	
DATE		o PAID / METHOD	
CUSTOMER		o SHIPPED	
		o CANCELLED	
ADDRESS		EST. SHIPPING DATE	
		SHIPPING COMPANY	
PHONE		TRACKING	
		SHIPPING DATE	
EMAIL		ARRIVAL DATE	

ITEM #	DESCRIPTION	QTY	PRICE	FINAL PRICE

NOTES	SUBTOTAL	
	DISCOUNT	
	TAXES	
	SHIPPING	
	GRAND TOTAL	

Order Form

ORDER #	
DATE	

CUSTOMER	
ADDRESS	
PHONE	
EMAIL	

STATUS	
o PAID / METHOD	
o SHIPPED	
o CANCELLED	
EST. SHIPPING DATE	
SHIPPING COMPANY	
TRACKING	
SHIPPING DATE	
ARRIVAL DATE	

ITEM #	DESCRIPTION	QTY	PRICE	FINAL PRICE

NOTES

SUBTOTAL	
DISCOUNT	
TAXES	
SHIPPING	
GRAND TOTAL	

Order Form

ORDER #	
DATE	

CUSTOMER	
ADDRESS	
PHONE	
EMAIL	

STATUS	
o PAID / METHOD	
o SHIPPED	
o CANCELLED	
EST. SHIPPING DATE	
SHIPPING COMPANY	
TRACKING	
SHIPPING DATE	
ARRIVAL DATE	

ITEM #	DESCRIPTION	QTY	PRICE	FINAL PRICE

NOTES		SUBTOTAL	
		DISCOUNT	
		TAXES	
		SHIPPING	
		GRAND TOTAL	

Order Form

ORDER #	
DATE	

CUSTOMER	
ADDRESS	
PHONE	
EMAIL	

STATUS	
o PAID / METHOD	
o SHIPPED	
o CANCELLED	
EST. SHIPPING DATE	
SHIPPING COMPANY	
TRACKING	
SHIPPING DATE	
ARRIVAL DATE	

ITEM #	DESCRIPTION	QTY	PRICE	FINAL PRICE

NOTES		
	SUBTOTAL	
	DISCOUNT	
	TAXES	
	SHIPPING	
	GRAND TOTAL	

Order Form

ORDER #	
DATE	

CUSTOMER	
ADDRESS	
PHONE	
EMAIL	

STATUS	
o PAID / METHOD	
o SHIPPED	
o CANCELLED	
EST. SHIPPING DATE	
SHIPPING COMPANY	
TRACKING	
SHIPPING DATE	
ARRIVAL DATE	

ITEM #	DESCRIPTION	QTY	PRICE	FINAL PRICE

NOTES		SUBTOTAL	
		DISCOUNT	
		TAXES	
		SHIPPING	
		GRAND TOTAL	

Order Form

ORDER #	
DATE	

CUSTOMER	
ADDRESS	
PHONE	
EMAIL	

STATUS	
o PAID / METHOD	
o SHIPPED	
o CANCELLED	
EST. SHIPPING DATE	
SHIPPING COMPANY	
TRACKING	
SHIPPING DATE	
ARRIVAL DATE	

ITEM #	DESCRIPTION	QTY	PRICE	FINAL PRICE

NOTES	SUBTOTAL	
	DISCOUNT	
	TAXES	
	SHIPPING	
	GRAND TOTAL	

Order Form

ORDER #	
DATE	

CUSTOMER	
ADDRESS	
PHONE	
EMAIL	

STATUS	
o PAID / METHOD	
o SHIPPED	
o CANCELLED	
EST. SHIPPING DATE	
SHIPPING COMPANY	
TRACKING	
SHIPPING DATE	
ARRIVAL DATE	

ITEM #	DESCRIPTION	QTY	PRICE	FINAL PRICE

NOTES

SUBTOTAL	
DISCOUNT	
TAXES	
SHIPPING	
GRAND TOTAL	

Order Form

ORDER #	
DATE	

CUSTOMER	
ADDRESS	
PHONE	
EMAIL	

STATUS	
o PAID / METHOD	
o SHIPPED	
o CANCELLED	
EST. SHIPPING DATE	
SHIPPING COMPANY	
TRACKING	
SHIPPING DATE	
ARRIVAL DATE	

ITEM #	DESCRIPTION	QTY	PRICE	FINAL PRICE

NOTES		SUBTOTAL	
		DISCOUNT	
		TAXES	
		SHIPPING	
		GRAND TOTAL	

Order Form

ORDER #	
DATE	

CUSTOMER	
ADDRESS	
PHONE	
EMAIL	

STATUS		
o PAID / METHOD		
o SHIPPED		
o CANCELLED		
EST. SHIPPING DATE		
SHIPPING COMPANY		
TRACKING		
SHIPPING DATE		
ARRIVAL DATE		

ITEM #	DESCRIPTION	QTY	PRICE	FINAL PRICE

NOTES	SUBTOTAL	
	DISCOUNT	
	TAXES	
	SHIPPING	
	GRAND TOTAL	

Order Form

ORDER #	
DATE	

CUSTOMER	
ADDRESS	
PHONE	
EMAIL	

STATUS	
o PAID / METHOD	
o SHIPPED	
o CANCELLED	
EST. SHIPPING DATE	
SHIPPING COMPANY	
TRACKING	
SHIPPING DATE	
ARRIVAL DATE	

ITEM #	DESCRIPTION	QTY	PRICE	FINAL PRICE

NOTES

SUBTOTAL	
DISCOUNT	
TAXES	
SHIPPING	
GRAND TOTAL	

Order Form

ORDER #	
DATE	

CUSTOMER	
ADDRESS	
PHONE	
EMAIL	

STATUS	
o PAID / METHOD	
o SHIPPED	
o CANCELLED	
EST. SHIPPING DATE	
SHIPPING COMPANY	
TRACKING	
SHIPPING DATE	
ARRIVAL DATE	

ITEM #	DESCRIPTION	QTY	PRICE	FINAL PRICE

NOTES	SUBTOTAL	
	DISCOUNT	
	TAXES	
	SHIPPING	
	GRAND TOTAL	

Order Form

ORDER #	
DATE	

CUSTOMER	
ADDRESS	
PHONE	
EMAIL	

STATUS	
o PAID / METHOD	
o SHIPPED	
o CANCELLED	
EST. SHIPPING DATE	
SHIPPING COMPANY	
TRACKING	
SHIPPING DATE	
ARRIVAL DATE	

ITEM #	DESCRIPTION	QTY	PRICE	FINAL PRICE

NOTES	SUBTOTAL	
	DISCOUNT	
	TAXES	
	SHIPPING	
	GRAND TOTAL	

Order Form

ORDER #	
DATE	

CUSTOMER	
ADDRESS	
PHONE	
EMAIL	

STATUS	
o PAID / METHOD	
o SHIPPED	
o CANCELLED	
EST. SHIPPING DATE	
SHIPPING COMPANY	
TRACKING	
SHIPPING DATE	
ARRIVAL DATE	

ITEM #	DESCRIPTION	QTY	PRICE	FINAL PRICE

NOTES		SUBTOTAL	
		DISCOUNT	
		TAXES	
		SHIPPING	
		GRAND TOTAL	

Order Form

ORDER #	
DATE	

CUSTOMER	
ADDRESS	
PHONE	
EMAIL	

STATUS	
o PAID / METHOD	
o SHIPPED	
o CANCELLED	
EST. SHIPPING DATE	
SHIPPING COMPANY	
TRACKING	
SHIPPING DATE	
ARRIVAL DATE	

ITEM #	DESCRIPTION	QTY	PRICE	FINAL PRICE

NOTES	SUBTOTAL	
	DISCOUNT	
	TAXES	
	SHIPPING	
	GRAND TOTAL	

Order Form

ORDER #	
DATE	

CUSTOMER	
ADDRESS	
PHONE	
EMAIL	

STATUS	
o PAID / METHOD	
o SHIPPED	
o CANCELLED	
EST. SHIPPING DATE	
SHIPPING COMPANY	
TRACKING	
SHIPPING DATE	
ARRIVAL DATE	

ITEM #	DESCRIPTION	QTY	PRICE	FINAL PRICE

NOTES		SUBTOTAL	
		DISCOUNT	
		TAXES	
		SHIPPING	
		GRAND TOTAL	

Order Form

ORDER #		STATUS	
DATE		o PAID / METHOD	
CUSTOMER		o SHIPPED	
		o CANCELLED	
ADDRESS		EST. SHIPPING DATE	
		SHIPPING COMPANY	
PHONE		TRACKING	
		SHIPPING DATE	
EMAIL		ARRIVAL DATE	

ITEM #	DESCRIPTION	QTY	PRICE	FINAL PRICE

NOTES		
	SUBTOTAL	
	DISCOUNT	
	TAXES	
	SHIPPING	
	GRAND TOTAL	

Order Form

ORDER #	
DATE	

CUSTOMER	
ADDRESS	
PHONE	
EMAIL	

STATUS	
o PAID / METHOD	
o SHIPPED	
o CANCELLED	
EST. SHIPPING DATE	
SHIPPING COMPANY	
TRACKING	
SHIPPING DATE	
ARRIVAL DATE	

ITEM #	DESCRIPTION	QTY	PRICE	FINAL PRICE

NOTES

SUBTOTAL	
DISCOUNT	
TAXES	
SHIPPING	
GRAND TOTAL	

Order Form

ORDER #	
DATE	

CUSTOMER	
ADDRESS	
PHONE	
EMAIL	

STATUS	
o PAID / METHOD	
o SHIPPED	
o CANCELLED	
EST. SHIPPING DATE	
SHIPPING COMPANY	
TRACKING	
SHIPPING DATE	
ARRIVAL DATE	

ITEM #	DESCRIPTION	QTY	PRICE	FINAL PRICE

NOTES	SUBTOTAL	
	DISCOUNT	
	TAXES	
	SHIPPING	
	GRAND TOTAL	

Order Form

ORDER #	
DATE	

CUSTOMER	
ADDRESS	
PHONE	
EMAIL	

STATUS		
o PAID / METHOD		
o SHIPPED		
o CANCELLED		
EST. SHIPPING DATE		
SHIPPING COMPANY		
TRACKING		
SHIPPING DATE		
ARRIVAL DATE		

ITEM #	DESCRIPTION	QTY	PRICE	FINAL PRICE

NOTES	SUBTOTAL	
	DISCOUNT	
	TAXES	
	SHIPPING	
	GRAND TOTAL	

Order Form

ORDER #		STATUS	
DATE		o PAID / METHOD	
		o SHIPPED	
CUSTOMER		o CANCELLED	
		EST. SHIPPING DATE	
ADDRESS		SHIPPING COMPANY	
		TRACKING	
PHONE		SHIPPING DATE	
EMAIL		ARRIVAL DATE	

ITEM #	DESCRIPTION	QTY	PRICE	FINAL PRICE

NOTES		
	SUBTOTAL	
	DISCOUNT	
	TAXES	
	SHIPPING	
	GRAND TOTAL	

Order Form

ORDER #	
DATE	

CUSTOMER	
ADDRESS	
PHONE	
EMAIL	

STATUS	
o PAID / METHOD	
o SHIPPED	
o CANCELLED	
EST. SHIPPING DATE	
SHIPPING COMPANY	
TRACKING	
SHIPPING DATE	
ARRIVAL DATE	

ITEM #	DESCRIPTION	QTY	PRICE	FINAL PRICE

NOTES	SUBTOTAL	
	DISCOUNT	
	TAXES	
	SHIPPING	
	GRAND TOTAL	

Order Form

ORDER #	
DATE	

CUSTOMER	
ADDRESS	
PHONE	
EMAIL	

STATUS	
o PAID / METHOD	
o SHIPPED	
o CANCELLED	
EST. SHIPPING DATE	
SHIPPING COMPANY	
TRACKING	
SHIPPING DATE	
ARRIVAL DATE	

ITEM #	DESCRIPTION	QTY	PRICE	FINAL PRICE

NOTES		SUBTOTAL	
		DISCOUNT	
		TAXES	
		SHIPPING	
		GRAND TOTAL	

Order Form

ORDER #		STATUS	
DATE		o PAID / METHOD	
CUSTOMER		o SHIPPED	
		o CANCELLED	
ADDRESS		EST. SHIPPING DATE	
		SHIPPING COMPANY	
PHONE		TRACKING	
		SHIPPING DATE	
EMAIL		ARRIVAL DATE	

ITEM #	DESCRIPTION	QTY	PRICE	FINAL PRICE

NOTES		
	SUBTOTAL	
	DISCOUNT	
	TAXES	
	SHIPPING	
	GRAND TOTAL	

Order Form

ORDER #	
DATE	

CUSTOMER	
ADDRESS	
PHONE	
EMAIL	

STATUS	
o PAID / METHOD	
o SHIPPED	
o CANCELLED	
EST. SHIPPING DATE	
SHIPPING COMPANY	
TRACKING	
SHIPPING DATE	
ARRIVAL DATE	

ITEM #	DESCRIPTION	QTY	PRICE	FINAL PRICE

NOTES		SUBTOTAL	
		DISCOUNT	
		TAXES	
		SHIPPING	
		GRAND TOTAL	

Order Form

ORDER #		STATUS	
DATE		o PAID / METHOD	
CUSTOMER		o SHIPPED	
		o CANCELLED	
ADDRESS		EST. SHIPPING DATE	
		SHIPPING COMPANY	
PHONE		TRACKING	
		SHIPPING DATE	
EMAIL		ARRIVAL DATE	

ITEM #	DESCRIPTION	QTY	PRICE	FINAL PRICE

NOTES	SUBTOTAL	
	DISCOUNT	
	TAXES	
	SHIPPING	
	GRAND TOTAL	

Order Form

ORDER #	
DATE	

CUSTOMER	
ADDRESS	
PHONE	
EMAIL	

STATUS	
o PAID / METHOD	
o SHIPPED	
o CANCELLED	
EST. SHIPPING DATE	
SHIPPING COMPANY	
TRACKING	
SHIPPING DATE	
ARRIVAL DATE	

ITEM #	DESCRIPTION	QTY	PRICE	FINAL PRICE

NOTES		SUBTOTAL	
		DISCOUNT	
		TAXES	
		SHIPPING	
		GRAND TOTAL	

Order Form

ORDER #	
DATE	

CUSTOMER	
ADDRESS	
PHONE	
EMAIL	

STATUS	
o PAID / METHOD	
o SHIPPED	
o CANCELLED	
EST. SHIPPING DATE	
SHIPPING COMPANY	
TRACKING	
SHIPPING DATE	
ARRIVAL DATE	

ITEM #	DESCRIPTION	QTY	PRICE	FINAL PRICE

NOTES

SUBTOTAL	
DISCOUNT	
TAXES	
SHIPPING	
GRAND TOTAL	

Order Form

ORDER #	
DATE	

CUSTOMER	
ADDRESS	
PHONE	
EMAIL	

STATUS	
o PAID / METHOD	
o SHIPPED	
o CANCELLED	
EST. SHIPPING DATE	
SHIPPING COMPANY	
TRACKING	
SHIPPING DATE	
ARRIVAL DATE	

ITEM #	DESCRIPTION	QTY	PRICE	FINAL PRICE

NOTES

SUBTOTAL	
DISCOUNT	
TAXES	
SHIPPING	
GRAND TOTAL	

Order Form

ORDER #	
DATE	

CUSTOMER	
ADDRESS	
PHONE	
EMAIL	

STATUS	
o PAID / METHOD	
o SHIPPED	
o CANCELLED	
EST. SHIPPING DATE	
SHIPPING COMPANY	
TRACKING	
SHIPPING DATE	
ARRIVAL DATE	

ITEM #	DESCRIPTION	QTY	PRICE	FINAL PRICE

NOTES

SUBTOTAL	
DISCOUNT	
TAXES	
SHIPPING	
GRAND TOTAL	

Order Form

ORDER #	
DATE	

CUSTOMER	
ADDRESS	
PHONE	
EMAIL	

STATUS	
o PAID / METHOD	
o SHIPPED	
o CANCELLED	
EST. SHIPPING DATE	
SHIPPING COMPANY	
TRACKING	
SHIPPING DATE	
ARRIVAL DATE	

ITEM #	DESCRIPTION	QTY	PRICE	FINAL PRICE

NOTES		SUBTOTAL	
		DISCOUNT	
		TAXES	
		SHIPPING	
		GRAND TOTAL	

Order Form

ORDER #	
DATE	

CUSTOMER	
ADDRESS	
PHONE	
EMAIL	

STATUS		
o PAID / METHOD		
o SHIPPED		
o CANCELLED		
EST. SHIPPING DATE		
SHIPPING COMPANY		
TRACKING		
SHIPPING DATE		
ARRIVAL DATE		

ITEM #	DESCRIPTION	QTY	PRICE	FINAL PRICE

NOTES	SUBTOTAL	
	DISCOUNT	
	TAXES	
	SHIPPING	
	GRAND TOTAL	

Order Form

ORDER #	
DATE	

CUSTOMER	
ADDRESS	
PHONE	
EMAIL	

STATUS	
o PAID / METHOD	
o SHIPPED	
o CANCELLED	
EST. SHIPPING DATE	
SHIPPING COMPANY	
TRACKING	
SHIPPING DATE	
ARRIVAL DATE	

ITEM #	DESCRIPTION	QTY	PRICE	FINAL PRICE

NOTES	SUBTOTAL	
	DISCOUNT	
	TAXES	
	SHIPPING	
	GRAND TOTAL	

Order Form

ORDER #	
DATE	

CUSTOMER	
ADDRESS	
PHONE	
EMAIL	

STATUS		
o PAID / METHOD		
o SHIPPED		
o CANCELLED		
EST. SHIPPING DATE		
SHIPPING COMPANY		
TRACKING		
SHIPPING DATE		
ARRIVAL DATE		

ITEM #	DESCRIPTION	QTY	PRICE	FINAL PRICE

NOTES	SUBTOTAL	
	DISCOUNT	
	TAXES	
	SHIPPING	
	GRAND TOTAL	

Order Form

ORDER #			STATUS	
DATE			o PAID / METHOD	
CUSTOMER			o SHIPPED	
			o CANCELLED	
ADDRESS			EST. SHIPPING DATE	
			SHIPPING COMPANY	
PHONE			TRACKING	
			SHIPPING DATE	
EMAIL			ARRIVAL DATE	

ITEM #	DESCRIPTION	QTY	PRICE	FINAL PRICE

NOTES		SUBTOTAL	
		DISCOUNT	
		TAXES	
		SHIPPING	
		GRAND TOTAL	

Order Form

ORDER #	
DATE	

CUSTOMER	
ADDRESS	
PHONE	
EMAIL	

STATUS	
o PAID / METHOD	
o SHIPPED	
o CANCELLED	
EST. SHIPPING DATE	
SHIPPING COMPANY	
TRACKING	
SHIPPING DATE	
ARRIVAL DATE	

ITEM #	DESCRIPTION	QTY	PRICE	FINAL PRICE

NOTES

SUBTOTAL	
DISCOUNT	
TAXES	
SHIPPING	
GRAND TOTAL	

Order Form

ORDER #	
DATE	

CUSTOMER	
ADDRESS	
PHONE	
EMAIL	

STATUS	
o PAID / METHOD	
o SHIPPED	
o CANCELLED	
EST. SHIPPING DATE	
SHIPPING COMPANY	
TRACKING	
SHIPPING DATE	
ARRIVAL DATE	

ITEM #	DESCRIPTION	QTY	PRICE	FINAL PRICE

NOTES	SUBTOTAL	
	DISCOUNT	
	TAXES	
	SHIPPING	
	GRAND TOTAL	

Order Form

ORDER #	
DATE	

CUSTOMER	
ADDRESS	
PHONE	
EMAIL	

STATUS	
o PAID / METHOD	
o SHIPPED	
o CANCELLED	
EST. SHIPPING DATE	
SHIPPING COMPANY	
TRACKING	
SHIPPING DATE	
ARRIVAL DATE	

ITEM #	DESCRIPTION	QTY	PRICE	FINAL PRICE

NOTES	SUBTOTAL	
	DISCOUNT	
	TAXES	
	SHIPPING	
	GRAND TOTAL	

Order Form

ORDER #	
DATE	

CUSTOMER	
ADDRESS	
PHONE	
EMAIL	

STATUS	
o PAID / METHOD	
o SHIPPED	
o CANCELLED	
EST. SHIPPING DATE	
SHIPPING COMPANY	
TRACKING	
SHIPPING DATE	
ARRIVAL DATE	

ITEM #	DESCRIPTION	QTY	PRICE	FINAL PRICE

NOTES		SUBTOTAL	
		DISCOUNT	
		TAXES	
		SHIPPING	
		GRAND TOTAL	

Order Form

ORDER #	
DATE	

CUSTOMER	
ADDRESS	
PHONE	
EMAIL	

STATUS		
o PAID / METHOD		
o SHIPPED		
o CANCELLED		
EST. SHIPPING DATE		
SHIPPING COMPANY		
TRACKING		
SHIPPING DATE		
ARRIVAL DATE		

ITEM #	DESCRIPTION	QTY	PRICE	FINAL PRICE

NOTES	SUBTOTAL	
	DISCOUNT	
	TAXES	
	SHIPPING	
	GRAND TOTAL	

Order Form

ORDER #	
DATE	

CUSTOMER	
ADDRESS	
PHONE	
EMAIL	

STATUS	
o PAID / METHOD	
o SHIPPED	
o CANCELLED	
EST. SHIPPING DATE	
SHIPPING COMPANY	
TRACKING	
SHIPPING DATE	
ARRIVAL DATE	

ITEM #	DESCRIPTION	QTY	PRICE	FINAL PRICE

NOTES

SUBTOTAL	
DISCOUNT	
TAXES	
SHIPPING	
GRAND TOTAL	

Order Form

ORDER #	
DATE	

CUSTOMER	
ADDRESS	
PHONE	
EMAIL	

STATUS		
o PAID / METHOD		
o SHIPPED		
o CANCELLED		
EST. SHIPPING DATE		
SHIPPING COMPANY		
TRACKING		
SHIPPING DATE		
ARRIVAL DATE		

ITEM #	DESCRIPTION	QTY	PRICE	FINAL PRICE

NOTES	SUBTOTAL	
	DISCOUNT	
	TAXES	
	SHIPPING	
	GRAND TOTAL	

Order Form

ORDER #	
DATE	

STATUS	
o PAID / METHOD	
o SHIPPED	
o CANCELLED	

CUSTOMER	
ADDRESS	
PHONE	
EMAIL	

EST. SHIPPING DATE	
SHIPPING COMPANY	
TRACKING	
SHIPPING DATE	
ARRIVAL DATE	

ITEM #	DESCRIPTION	QTY	PRICE	FINAL PRICE

NOTES

SUBTOTAL	
DISCOUNT	
TAXES	
SHIPPING	
GRAND TOTAL	

Order Form

ORDER #	
DATE	

CUSTOMER	
ADDRESS	
PHONE	
EMAIL	

STATUS	
o PAID / METHOD	
o SHIPPED	
o CANCELLED	
EST. SHIPPING DATE	
SHIPPING COMPANY	
TRACKING	
SHIPPING DATE	
ARRIVAL DATE	

ITEM #	DESCRIPTION	QTY	PRICE	FINAL PRICE

NOTES	SUBTOTAL	
	DISCOUNT	
	TAXES	
	SHIPPING	
	GRAND TOTAL	

Order Form

ORDER #	
DATE	

CUSTOMER	
ADDRESS	
PHONE	
EMAIL	

STATUS	
o PAID / METHOD	
o SHIPPED	
o CANCELLED	
EST. SHIPPING DATE	
SHIPPING COMPANY	
TRACKING	
SHIPPING DATE	
ARRIVAL DATE	

ITEM #	DESCRIPTION	QTY	PRICE	FINAL PRICE

NOTES

SUBTOTAL	
DISCOUNT	
TAXES	
SHIPPING	
GRAND TOTAL	

Order Form

ORDER #	
DATE	

CUSTOMER	
ADDRESS	
PHONE	
EMAIL	

STATUS	
o PAID / METHOD	
o SHIPPED	
o CANCELLED	
EST. SHIPPING DATE	
SHIPPING COMPANY	
TRACKING	
SHIPPING DATE	
ARRIVAL DATE	

ITEM #	DESCRIPTION	QTY	PRICE	FINAL PRICE

NOTES

SUBTOTAL	
DISCOUNT	
TAXES	
SHIPPING	
GRAND TOTAL	

Order Form

ORDER #	
DATE	

CUSTOMER	
ADDRESS	
PHONE	
EMAIL	

STATUS	
o PAID / METHOD	
o SHIPPED	
o CANCELLED	
EST. SHIPPING DATE	
SHIPPING COMPANY	
TRACKING	
SHIPPING DATE	
ARRIVAL DATE	

ITEM #	DESCRIPTION	QTY	PRICE	FINAL PRICE

NOTES		SUBTOTAL	
		DISCOUNT	
		TAXES	
		SHIPPING	
		GRAND TOTAL	

Order Form

ORDER #	
DATE	

CUSTOMER	
ADDRESS	
PHONE	
EMAIL	

STATUS	
o PAID / METHOD	
o SHIPPED	
o CANCELLED	
EST. SHIPPING DATE	
SHIPPING COMPANY	
TRACKING	
SHIPPING DATE	
ARRIVAL DATE	

ITEM #	DESCRIPTION	QTY	PRICE	FINAL PRICE

NOTES	SUBTOTAL	
	DISCOUNT	
	TAXES	
	SHIPPING	
	GRAND TOTAL	

Order Form

ORDER #	
DATE	

CUSTOMER	
ADDRESS	
PHONE	
EMAIL	

STATUS	
o PAID / METHOD	
o SHIPPED	
o CANCELLED	
EST. SHIPPING DATE	
SHIPPING COMPANY	
TRACKING	
SHIPPING DATE	
ARRIVAL DATE	

ITEM #	DESCRIPTION	QTY	PRICE	FINAL PRICE

NOTES		SUBTOTAL	
		DISCOUNT	
		TAXES	
		SHIPPING	
		GRAND TOTAL	

Order Form

ORDER #	
DATE	

CUSTOMER	
ADDRESS	
PHONE	
EMAIL	

STATUS	
o PAID / METHOD	
o SHIPPED	
o CANCELLED	
EST. SHIPPING DATE	
SHIPPING COMPANY	
TRACKING	
SHIPPING DATE	
ARRIVAL DATE	

ITEM #	DESCRIPTION	QTY	PRICE	FINAL PRICE

NOTES		SUBTOTAL	
		DISCOUNT	
		TAXES	
		SHIPPING	
		GRAND TOTAL	

Order Form

ORDER #	
DATE	

STATUS	
o PAID / METHOD	
o SHIPPED	
o CANCELLED	

CUSTOMER	
ADDRESS	
PHONE	
EMAIL	

EST. SHIPPING DATE	
SHIPPING COMPANY	
TRACKING	
SHIPPING DATE	
ARRIVAL DATE	

ITEM #	DESCRIPTION	QTY	PRICE	FINAL PRICE

NOTES

SUBTOTAL	
DISCOUNT	
TAXES	
SHIPPING	
GRAND TOTAL	

Order Form

ORDER #	
DATE	

CUSTOMER	
ADDRESS	
PHONE	
EMAIL	

STATUS	
o PAID / METHOD	
o SHIPPED	
o CANCELLED	
EST. SHIPPING DATE	
SHIPPING COMPANY	
TRACKING	
SHIPPING DATE	
ARRIVAL DATE	

ITEM #	DESCRIPTION	QTY	PRICE	FINAL PRICE

NOTES	SUBTOTAL	
	DISCOUNT	
	TAXES	
	SHIPPING	
	GRAND TOTAL